JANE DOES NOT REMEMBER

WHO OR WHAT CAME FIRST

AHSAHTA PRESS
BOISE, IDAHO
2013

THE NEW SERIES
#53

FORTY-ONE JANE DOE'S

CARRIE OLIVIA ADAMS

Ahsahta Press, Boise State University, Boise, Idaho 83725-1525
ahsahtapress.org
Cover design by Quemadura
Book design by Janet Holmes
Printed in Canada

LIBRARY OF CONGRESS CATALOGING-IN-PUBLICATION DATA

Adams, Carrie Olivia.
Forty-one Jane Doe's / Carrie Olivia Adams.
p. cm.—(The new series ; 53)
Poems.
ISBN 978-1-934103-39-5 (pbk. : alk. paper)
ISBN 1-934103-39-X (pbk. : alk. paper)
I. Title.
PS3601.D3695F68 2015
811'.6—DC23
2012029813

ACKNOWLEDGMENTS

Many thanks to the editors of the journals where these poems first appeared, sometimes under slightly different titles: *Cannibal:* "Winter Came" (poem only); *Coconut:* "Pandora's Star Box" (poem only); *Dear Camera Magazine:* "The Lives of the Forty-One Jane Doe's" (poem & film); *The Laurel Review:* "A Mystery Story"; *Map Literary:* "Voice Made Small" and "Intermission with the Aviator"; Mare Nostrum: "Technologies"; *Slope:* "Winter Came" (film only); *Word / For Word:* "Intermission with Strings" (Previously called: "There Are Strings")

I am honored and humbled to be a part of Ahsahta's distinguished list of poets, and I am incredibly grateful to Janet Holmes for taking a chance on my first book, *Intervening Absence*—and now this, my second. Her enthusiasm and encouragement have been invaluable these past years. Similarly, I want to thank the friends who have been insightful early readers of the poems, creative companions, and empathetic cocktail drinkers—Janaka Stucky, Bill Rasmovicz, Levi Stahl, Jeannine Lyons, Jennifer Ringblom, and Joseph Clayton Mills. Along the way, I've been lucky to have Bob and Paula Ferguson, Betsy Wooten, and Ronnie Burchett as supportive family forces. And, of course, I send enormous love and gratitude to Taylor Adams, who cheers me through and is extremely patient with me throughout the writing process, often serves as my handy technical engineer at screenings, and mixes a mighty fine drink just when I need it.

CONTENTS

I   A Mystery Story

13   Pandora's Star Box

23   Intermission with the Scientist

29   Technologies

39   Intermission with the Aviator

43   Winter Came

53   Intermission with Strings

59   The Lives of the Forty-One Jane Doe's

71   Voice Made Small

Love is a sign of our badness.

SIMONE WEIL, *GRAVITY AND GRACE*

A MYSTERY STORY

She would begin by predicting the weather.

The first clue is snowflakes.

She gathers teeth
marks. Flesh torn. Hot.
Then cold to the touch.

No, the detective thinks.
Fabric fibers over ice crystals.
Fingernails.

This one delivered.
By hand. By beak.
By slow boat. By
tip toe.
By knocked over accident.

This clue is paper
wrapped. Her fingers
grapple with the seams.

The first clue is wide-eyed.
It is the departure.

Here's a hint.

The detective is accused of looking
so much like someone / anyone else.

She has one of those faces.

Left or leaving.

Do you have a memory?

Torn by her teeth.
Curled up in her brown hair.

She promises you—

She looks nothing like her.

The detective uncovers—

What would be common evidence—

                      the heart, the

blood—
And the failure of
Re-form / trans-form / pro-test
                / -ation
The body, if not guide.

The detective knows
If there was a window, you'd close it
to keep out the smell of urban wakefulness.
Or decay. The neighbors.
Or the fireworks—

                    the clouds that remain
                    And drift in their shape.

She knows you've found this
trace, and didn't tell her.

Another clue in the street
after it has been swept.
And it's just the pigeons and her
picking at the crumbs
too small
to sweep.

It snows when the sun is out.

It's true that there is no lack.
Or that the abundance
has become its own lack
of wonder

for the detective.
Each bird carries a piece.

That scratching over her shoulder,
that boney beak against pavement—

She is not alone here, seeking

or other.

The Detective has a pornographic mouth.
So she's been told.
So she uses it.

She begs. She pouts.
She swallows / lies.

It might be criminal.

Sometimes she scavenges for fantasies
and leaves her own clues lying
                  and lain.

Moments after asking
what is the meaning of love
she makes love.

This does not answer
the question.

How does she explain—

If she were braver
She would have understood
that one could take suffering

(is it a clue?)

and make a life.

The detective has a whole list that begins:
If I were braver.

(is this the mystery)

If she were braver, she would ask:
Can lies be a form of compassion?

The truth (a clue? a mystery?)—

She spares you with a spare truth.

Some days there are no clues
other than the patterns of migrating birds.

She read that in autumn the skyscrapers
are a hindrance to the determined
                              but clumsy.
And there is a hospital in the park:
if you find a robin or a sparrow on the sidewalk,
you can carry it to their hands and stethoscopes.

She remembers a thud
and gray feathers stuck to the window.
                              It took hours for them to blow away.

She did not find a body.

In many clues there was a draught
and even the pavement cracked
in wide-mouthed begging
until the rain burst
and she briefly forgot
that she had been wanting.

There is a saintly service
she holds on her tongue.
The tongue weighs it.

It was the idea that held you here.

The detective
       she leaves it to you.

PANDORA'S STAR BOX

Even if there is only one possible unified theory, it is just a set of rules and equations. What is it that breathes fire into the equations and makes a universe for them to describe? The usual approach of science of constructing a mathematical model cannot answer the questions of why there should be a universe for the model to describe. Why does the universe go to all the bother of existing?

STEPHEN HAWKING, *A BRIEF HISTORY OF TIME*

You wrote:

Sometimes I think the sky itself might be one of my fantasies. I've never touched it.

Dear Astronomer,

I felt it in the lake. The water lay motionless, silent, waiting. It was patient. And the sky was seduced there. The clouds lay upon the water. I placed my fingertips into them. I touched the verge.

I kept it to myself.

My secrets make me small. I share this with your stars. In their distance, which makes them small, they are secret keepers too. You must think they whisper to each other when you're not looking. Or even when you are. How could you really tell? That light. They burn their undelivered letters to you. But in this interiority. Of mine. And theirs. There is an opening in. This opening, a unit of measure. A handbook. A handbreadth. A reach.

Dear Astronomer,

I opened the box. It was me. There was no lock or key. I just asked, "Shall I?"

And the stars fell out.

There was a universe before and after me.

Then, I reclaimed the box.

To explain, I have given the box a window. To become perceptible; to be expressed; to permit passage; to make manifest. Maybe for all these reasons. It caught a cluster, a bee and a thistle; the spindle of a watch balance. The sun on the tip of a matchstick.

I tell you I would like to put it all back inside. The entire globe and its halo.

I've settled for having the universe both within and outside the box.

You wrote: *Number is the within of all things.*

A tin and tiny time coded message.

I have spied over your shoulder, dear Astronomer. I've green eyed the tables and the grids you build. They are my steep edges and skin-rubbed cliff face. You have built a vocabulary in which crisis is the opposite of catastrophe. You mean to tell me that the turning point is not necessarily the final event. I want to listen. I want to believe that the stars are an opening out.

I want to.

It's not so vast, I want you to know. When I look out I can trap it between my eyelids.
Clutch the sun as it flickers on dark water.

It's archaic, but curious can simply mean to be made carefully. Is that it? An attentive but solicitous opening? The peaks breaking the line of the sky.

Dear Astronomer,

What do you do during the daylight? Do you train your telescope on people across the way? Are you curious at all about earthly perambulations? Do you chart them—map them—trace them from point to point with a protractor in the same way?

I once wrote to you and asked—why do people make love? It was a foolish question, I know.

This box traps and releases desire. There are lots of names for desire, like greed and envy and longing and hope, but they are all desire. It's the same seashore. The same fisherman. The same afternoon that splashes light and fades heavy.

I don't know why this one or that one. But I know desire.

You wrote: *geometry is knowledge of the eternally existent*.
Astronomer, I know you're curious about fire—
You divide the stars into snow globes and sun shades.

And in between word from you the chattering of my teeth passes as
small talk between us.

We both go to the high places. The sudden ones. The serrated ones.
The ones that are the last line that we can find between land and sky.

You are closer. And I am further.

All those gifts squandered, the constellations must think of me. Of us.

Dear Astronomer, you must be versed in death and know that so much is dimming that we cannot see yet. You know that this light that is our sky may have already disappeared.

Does it seem strange to you that the stars are a record of earthly feats by heavenly beings? There are 18 moons of Saturn, and I am one of them.

Yet, I am ashamed to spend time worrying about the stars burning themselves into darkness. Perhaps it is because everything else has already fallen. I have had a hand in it. No amount of dipping into lakes and seas has drowned that.

I want to ask you to make this vessel, this body, my sin. I have carried it across this earth. If not across your sky.

You've sat nightly and watched what I've put forth.
Astronomer, you tell me, *there is geometry in the humming of strings.*

I've said it is all bird calls echoing in a cave.

You tell me—Make the blue a little more blue.

I've touched it, I tell you.
   It was all there once:
   Seduced for a moment
      and it breathed light.

INTERMISSION WITH THE SCIENTIST

I have with the aid of a magnifying glass
both seen the heart
pulsating myself
and shown it
to many others.

The heart rises upwards
to a point
so that as it strikes
against the breast
the pulse is felt externally.

I've grown tired of my heart—
it knows not its place.

My heart being grasped
in the hand, is felt
to become harder
during its action.

Shhh. Quiet little heart.

The heart, my heart,
when it moves,
becomes of a paler color,
when quiescent
it is red.

In the pause
the heart is soft,
exhausted, lying,
as it were
at rest.

He watched it.
He didn't know
whether to bandage it
and let it heal
or let it out the window.

Once, with a pigeon,
after the heart had ceased,
he wetted his finger with saliva;
and warm for a short time
upon the heart,
both ventricles and auricles pulsated.

TECHNOLOGIES

It was awkward, but it fitted me.

[In real life]

My body.
        Reader,
he strokes it in letters.

In those < stories
it is a silhouette—

It feels as much me as this > hand,

which I should tell you, reader, feels like it came from somewhere else:

I don't know how to return it [if I wanted to].

On the other < hand

[in real life]

it pretends it were him.

Always already a clone.

Reader, you and I have been lashed
by the weather. We've been let down.
The glass served as a transfer point.
The more in here moved
to the less out there.
Or tried.
And gathered just the same.

At the top of the mountain,

       the peak

              is one breath wide.

    As soon as my voice cracks,

      He can measure——

      It is one second from bliss

              to loss.

The clutter of < crucibles > is our busy work.

In the space between letters.

Technologies: bread, pantomime, seduction, tongue tying.

I don't know what to say about him.
He is no longer a phantasm,
But not yet a sign.

The seagulls have taken residence
in the grocery parking lot.
Their squawks and squeals
each morning circling the block.

He lives by the ocean.
There is just a pretend one here.
There is a beach. And I can stand there
on the edge amid the wind and wave breaks
and say to myself: "I am at the ocean."

Perhaps he has sent the gulls
to pretend with me.
That would be a sign. A recognition.
That's the kind of thing he'd do.

Do you know mathematical beauty, reader?

Pure equation.

Identity $<$ to bind the constants.

It ends: $+ 1 = 0$

This holds the world together.

I've been told.

[in mathematical life]

I try to imagine the space without me in it.
First the bed, then the train car, the coffee line.

It is an act of extreme egotism to believe
that my being [here]
changes the city.
Disrupts it so.
A windbreak. A shadow caster.
My breath catches. Extends.

Self or selfless,
I am in the way.

In one of our stories,
afterward, when we lie apart
I tell him that my mind
feels distant now from my wrists,
knee caps, the hinges.

[in either life]

The refracted image of a sea caught
 still sleeping.

INTERMISSION WITH THE AVIATOR

The sky grew white with birds
She had told you that you could never take flight.

[blink]

The feathers fell
Revealing only the moon behind them.

[blink]

She had meant that you would thrash in the ocean
And not feel your feet leave the water.

[blink]

She had tried to leave her body behind.
But it would not stay.

As she moved towards you, it too arose from the pillows
Leaving an impression of where it had been.

[blink]

Her fingertips dug in
What had seemed like air was flesh.

Now, when she sees your
name it is your body.
It takes shape as you.

[blink]

A jade seal or a curving lip
An expression [blink]

That from these heights
Is as much terror as pledge.

[blink]

WINTER CAME

This was the year I deserved the winter,
and when it came there was nothing
            I could say—
I could not send it back.

It had come for me.

The pipes below the street burst,
the locks froze.
In the dark, as it seemed always,
men huddled deeper into entryways
        building blankets from plastic and rags.

It was my fault:
        The winter was mine

One night I was awakened by the building breaking,
the ceiling collapsed,
the roof opened to reveal the sky
        yawning back at me—

                echoing my escapist sleep.

When the winter came
I thought it might never leave us;
        or would never leave without me.

I began to plot how I might wrap myself
        in it / send myself back:
                beg a sparrow's wing
                a pomegranate's ride.

This was the year I was spider bitten;
        the venom began at my fingers, and
each hand kept moving to touch the other
        fearing they might freeze in motion.

It traveled as an icy fog
        through the veins of my wrists.
This was the winter
I studied each blue timber,
but the map of my body gave no sign of a route or causeway.

Yet, it was reason you begged for
which became one more breath withheld.

I realized later that there must have been sun,
        but I had forgotten it.
The church was sinking,
        the snow melted in cracks from above.

I tried to will my lungs not to move;
        my heart to lie still, warm under layers.

Why must the body insist?

That which is enough
      to make me believe
is the very same thing
that makes me believe
      he is distant / or has forgotten me.

Buoyant, but I could drown it.
      Faith / that is the ocean
      the floor.

Why for
a whisp / a purr
           this whip / this wind
this sounds that meets its echo
      in graffiti from strangers.

It was a man's voice
      in my ear.
How many times I had heard this pleading
      before the winter came.

There was that time / longer than a moment,
long enough to watch the frost build

                              upon the window
one thinly drawn molecule / branch at a time.

That night when we couldn't tell
            whether it was the train
or the wind we were hearing.

                        And it was both.

And we were in bed,
and I wanted to tell you;
            I opened my mouth to tell you.
And you were asleep
so I waited some more in the winter / my winter.

                        And off and on, one of us was sleeping.

In the end
this cold glass
waiting for us.

Before there was this memory
      empathy was imagining the empty spaces
                    pity /seeing them.

            Cursed to be so blessed
            I begged you to beat me.

            What more evidence do you need
that we've been given up.

The sky gapes—
        to pull us out?

A cruel, characteristic gesture
when it came.

It is heavy
      under this winter.

Forgive me,

I have thinned
the skin from the bite

and watched the moon
fade to shadow
and done nothing
      but throw fire against the glass / to see its reflection.

My winter would not leave me—
      It made me watch instead.

INTERMISSION WITH STRINGS

If I could thread
a needle and begin to stitch
together the smallest I could find—

an eyelash, a fingerprint—
it would be like writing a letter:

I don't know how to close
a door, but I am sending
the sound of it latching.

The photo that caught you
collective, the years of

history, small but heavy.

If I could remove the stone before the door:

dovecote
columbarium
hotel room—

Would we enter
and stay small forever.

In the theory of everything,
there are strings
and the vibrations
of strings.

If I'm not small
enough, we can start thinking
of what to remove.

Maybe then we can fold
these words upon themselves?

A pigeon hole
an apiary
a catacomb:

this pinprick.

A vibrating tendon—mine,
you pluck it. String of a cello bass.

Snip it, and
I would no longer be afraid;
even when I should be.

THE LIVES OF THE FORTY-ONE JANE DOE'S

There are Janes for everyday.

And there are sometime Janes.

There are Janes that are only noticed when they wear red.

"Hey, Red!"

    "Red!"

    The man on the corner calls out Jane by her dress. He doesn't know

        she's a Jane.

You may have fucked a Jane and didn't know it.

    "God damn," you called.

      And Jane answered.

If there were Forty-one Jane Doe's crowded in a graffitied bathroom stall—

      They would all be dialing one number.

Voices on the line would say:

I want you to have no bad memories, Jane.

Jane, everyone but you seems to know that memories are the consolation prize.

Mornings, Jane tries to look so tall,
no matter what she's carrying.
She strides down the wooden train platform, one hand
holding her skirt against the breeze, the other clutching.

If they look, and some days they do,
she thinks it must be because her steps are too loud.
Or they must be looking past her, down the tracks.

She does not know where to set her eyes, and
Jane can't help feeling guilty for remembering anything at all.

The Janes sprang from monuments.
From city plans; from bridge blue prints.

One day there were high rise office buildings
and tenements and grids
and alleyways sunk under with rain water.
And the Janes came with them.

Click clacking across the pavement,
sidestepping subway grates,
their heeled teetering, a miraculous scene:

Amid this nonstop flock of lookers,
witnesses in tow,
children, lovers, would be
Janets, Jills, and Johns—

All women warn you that they are trouble,
but the Janes mean it.
(Though they'll apologize afterward.)

One Jane spent a long time sitting on the vanity.
Her feet in the sink;
her body pulled into a ball;
her face nearly touching the mirror glass.
Jane stared eye to eye,
but could not match her mind to the body—
Was she faced with yet another Jane?

This Jane was old enough to know
that she could not reach through the glass,
place her hands around the neck of the other Jane
and demand answers.

This Jane was old enough to feel herself
mulling it over with her lip.
And watched the other Jane doing the same.
Tearing the skin back and forth across her front teeth.

There was something between them,
even if just a gesture.

There is a legend
that the Janes' forty-one bodies have worn them soft,
and rubbed them white.

Still
they could use those sheets
                    to make a rope.

Scale the statues,
the architectural facades.
Would they then be for climbing out
or in.

Yet the bed pillows would smother,
and all the threads they had bitten
                        between their teeth,
could be caught in the Janes' throats.

The Janes play opossum.
They practice their absence sometimes.
They could be putting you on,
but then again—

One Jane Doe remembers burying
Jane Doe in the sand.

There is a moment, she says,
when you know what you are doing
is wrong, but you do it anyway.
This does not mean
that you do not have remorse.
You feel more guilt
for having done it

anyway.

The Janes are still moving through the city.
They are throwing seeds out bus windows,
planting fallow corners and medians.

The Janes have hands in their pockets,
fumbling bump keys.
They know how to break-in
and rearrange the furniture.

Jane knows that streetlight is going to go out
just when she's bending over to pick up the paper.

God Jane—your fingers when you think of them.

There is a voice in her head that tells her
she is a monster.
Jane is told to ignore it,
which she thinks would be easy,
if the voice were wrong.

Jane does not remember
who or what came first.

The sinner and then the saint,
it keeps repeating.

God damn Jane.

Doe-eyed Jane begs for brandy.
It's for the aching in her jaw.

She's ground her teeth into chalk.
Her tongue rolled in white powder and grit
is the last thing Jane sees before falling asleep.

She's heard the grinding in her dreams.
The cogs of a life slow moving,
rubbing against each other.
Bone upon bone.
Coarse and dry,
a brittle spit foam.

This is what they've done to each other.

The Janes are truss and joint
they distribute the shear and bending.
They've been holding it up.

They are going to age.
Maybe with grace,
maybe with gravity.

It is the sin in me that says I.
The good gets broken up into pieces and scattered.
The Janes are no respectable idol.
They'll wander off.
They'll find the trap doors and the cement cracks.
They get tired.

Somedays, there's got to be a way to save Jane.

You may have loved a Jane and didn't know it.
Some passionate sleepwalker, arms outstretched,
the dust falling, the pollen grains,
if the Janes were buried, quietly,
only later, the foundation rustles.

VOICE MADE SMALL

My voice made small
travels with others
along the copper wires.

Then, there is the sea—
I do not know how sound travels
across it.

The tips of the waves,
moths that flutter toward your ears.

There is the sea—
It could carry us.
It could lose us.

Once there was a paper mill.
I brought them your letters
and your letters became
paper again.

Your voice becomes water again.

When you wrote the story
of the end
(of the world, was it?)

I was measuring the weather;
tying balloons
to the feet of pigeons
on the sidewalk.

There is a story
of a man from LA
who took flight with his lawn
chair
and 45 weather balloons.
He became untethered.

The waves are still tethered,
I think.
The moon, its light,
recalls them
if we cannot.

If you know the end,
if the day has already come
and another begun for you
can you tell me of it,
so I may know
what to look for?

NOTES

PANDORA'S STAR BOX

"Number is the within of all things," "Geometry is knowledge of the eternally existent," and "There is geometry in the humming of strings" are all borrowed from Pythagoras.

INTERMISSION WITH THE SCIENTIST

Refers to an experiment involving a pigeon described by William Harvey (1510–90) in *On the Motion of the Heart and Blood in Animals*.

TECHNOLOGIES

References an equation by Swiss mathematician and physicist Leonard Euler (1707–83). Euler's identity theorem $e^{i\pi} + 1 = 0$, used in trigonometry, is often described by mathematicians as "the most beautiful equation," due to the fact that three basic arithmetic operations occur exactly once each: addition, multiplication, and exponentiation, and the theorem links five fundamental mathematical constants.

INTERMISSION WITH STRINGS

Also makes reference to the quote from Pythagoras: "There is geometry in the humming of the strings. There is music in the spacings of the spheres."

THE LIVES OF THE FORTY-ONE JANE DOE'S

Was inspired by the Forty One Jane Doe's cocktail at the Violet Hour in Chicago and is dedicated to its bartenders. It also alludes to passages in *Gravity and Grace* by Simone Weil (1909–43).

ABOUT THE AUTHOR

CARRIE OLIVIA ADAMS lives in Chicago, where she is a book publicist for the University of Chicago Press and the poetry editor for the small press Black Ocean. She is the author of *Intervening Absence,* also published by Ahsahta Press.

AHSAHTA PRESS

SAWTOOTH POETRY PRIZE SERIES

2002: Aaron McCollough, *Welkin* (Brenda Hillman, judge)

2003: Graham Foust, *Leave the Room to Itself* (Joe Wenderoth, judge)

2004: Noah Eli Gordon, *The Area of Sound Called the Subtone* (Claudia Rankine, judge)

2005: Karla Kelsey, *Knowledge, Forms, The Aviary* (Carolyn Forché, judge)

2006: Paige Ackerson-Kiely, *In No One's Land* (D. A. Powell, judge)

2007: Rusty Morrison, *the true keeps calm biding its story* (Peter Gizzi, judge)

2008: Barbara Maloutas, *the whole Marie* (C. D. Wright, judge)

2009: Julie Carr, *100 Notes on Violence* (Rae Armantrout, judge)

2010: James Meetze, *Dayglo* (Terrance Hayes, judge)

2011: Karen Rigby, *Chinoiserie* (Paul Hoover, judge)

2012: T. Zachary Cotler, *Sonnets to the Humans* (Heather McHugh, judge)

AHSAHTA PRESS

NEW SERIES

1. Lance Phillips, *Corpus Socius*
2. Heather Sellers, *Drinking Girls and Their Dresses*
3. Lisa Fishman, *Dear, Read*
4. Peggy Hamilton, *Forbidden City*
5. Dan Beachy-Quick, *Spell*
6. Liz Waldner, *Saving the Appearances*
7. Charles O. Hartman, *Island*
8. Lance Phillips, *Cur aliquid vidi*
9. Sandra Miller, *oriflamme.*
10. Brigitte Byrd, *Fence Above the Sea*
11. Ethan Paquin, *The Violence*
12. Ed Allen, *67 Mixed Messages*
13. Brian Henry, *Quarantine*
14. Kate Greenstreet, *case sensitive*
15. Aaron McCollough, *Little Ease*
16. Susan Tichy, *Bone Pagoda*
17. Susan Briante, *Pioneers in the Study of Motion*
18. Lisa Fishman, *The Happiness Experiment*
19. Heidi Lynn Staples, *Dog Girl*
20. David Mutschlecner, *Sign*
21. Kristi Maxwell, *Realm Sixty-four*
22. G. E. Patterson, *To and From*
23. Chris Vitiello, *Irresponsibility*
24. Stephanie Strickland, *Zone : Zero*
25. Charles O. Hartman, *New and Selected Poems*
26. Kathleen Jesme, *The Plum-Stone Game*
27. Ben Doller, *FAQ:*
28. Carrie Olivia Adams, *Intervening Absence*
29. Rachel Loden, *Dick of the Dead*
30. Brigitte Byrd, *Song of a Living Room*
31. Kate Greenstreet, *The Last 4 Things*
32. Brenda Iijima, *If Not Metamorphic*
33. Sandra Doller, *Chora.*
34. Susan Tichy, *Gallowglass*
35. Lance Phillips, *These Indicium Tales*
36. Karla Kelsey, *Iteration Nets*
37. Brian Teare, *Pleasure*
38. Kristen Kaschock, *A Beautiful Name for a Girl*
39. Susan Briante, *Utopia Minus*
40. Brian Henry, *Lessness*
41. Lisa Fishman, *FLOWER CART*
42. Aaron McCollough, *No Grave Can Hold My Body Down*
43. Kristi Maxwell, *Re-*
44. Andrew Grace, *Sancta*
45. Chris Vitiello, *Obedience*
46. Paige Ackerson-Kiely, *My Love Is a Dead Arctic Explorer*
47. David Mutschlecner, *Enigma and Light*
48. Joshua Corey and G.C. Waldrep, eds., *The Arcadia Project*
49. Dan Beachy-Quick and Matthew Goulish, *Work from Memory*
50. Elizabeth Robinson, *Counterpart*
51. Kate Greenstreet, *Young Tambling*
52. Ethan Paquin, *Cloud vs. Cloud*
53. Carrie Olivia Adams, *Forty-one Jane Does*

This book is set in Apollo MT type
with Titling Gothic FB Skyline titles
by Ahsahta Press at Boise State University.
Cover design by Quemadura.
Book design by Janet Holmes.
Printed in Canada.

AHSAHTA PRESS

2013

JANET HOLMES, DIRECTOR

CHRISTOPHER CARUSO   RYAN HOLMAN

JODI CHILSON   MELISSA HUGHES, *intern*

KYLE CRAWFORD   TORIN JENSEN

CHARLES GABEL   ANNIE KNOWLES

JESSICA HAMBLETON, *intern*   STEPHA PETERS

JULIE STRAND